CRIME, SOCIETY AND CONSCIENCE

COLUMBA EXPLORATIONS 3

Crime, Society and Conscience

Edited by

Seán MacRéamoinn

the columba press

First published in 1997 by
the columba press
55A Spruce Avenue, Stillorgan Industrial Park,
Blackrock, Co Dublin

Cover by Bill Bolger
Origination by The Columba Press
Printed in Ireland by Genprint Ltd, Dublin

ISBN 1 85607 189 8

Contents

CHAPTER 1

Moral Breakdown?

Seán MacRéamoinn

It is, I believe, fair to say that, until comparatively recently, the word *moral* and its derivatives were commonly understood as having to do with sex. To the point that it was alleged that Irish Catholics took only one kind of sin really seriously: killing, stealing, perjury and so on were certainly against God's law, but they could sometimes be excused, while adultery and fornication and even 'bad thoughts' were gravely wrong, always and everywhere.

While this was a caricature of Catholic teaching and practice, there can be little doubt that it reflected, however distortedly, an all too common attitude. But, it should be recognised that this attitude was not to be found only among Catholics, nor was it uniquely Irish. It was believed, however unfairly, to be a hallmark of all 'religious' societies, especially those where the prevailing ethos appeared to derive from Puritanism: it was certainly a dominant feature of what became known as Victorianism, and not just in those lands owing allegiance to the good Queen herself. And, returning home, it became a kind of common ground held by 'respectable' people, Protestant and Catholic, north and south, in the second half of the nineteenth century, surviving well into the first half of the twentieth.

There were of course some differences. Protestant morality stressed the importance of personal honesty, as well as a strict observance of the commandment to keep the Sabbath holy. Among Catholics, regular church-going and Friday abstinence were religious duties of social, not to say public, consequence. All of which, of course, is not to say that respectable Protestants were lax in church-going, or that their Catholic peers were not insistent on the sacredness of property. But sexual morality was the social value *par excellence*, esteemed on all sides. Divergences in the actual code of sexual behaviour developed only in this century, especially after the first world war, when divorce began to achieve a certain respectability among Protestants, and later, when Lambeth and Rome differed sharply and publicly on the question of 'family planning'.

But in 1950 as in 1850, from Belfast to Ballycotton, if a man, or a woman, came to earn the stigma of leading 'an immoral life' it could be taken that the offence was of a blatant sexual nature. One would never so describe a bad employer, or a shopkeeper who consistently gave short weight, or a notorious gossip and scandal-monger, or a wife-beater, or a sadistic teacher, or an avaricious priest. None of these, however reprehensible their behaviour, had offended against morality!

Whether we would judge such persons today as guilty of immoral behaviour is not quite the point: what is important is that we have come to recognise that morality has much wider and deeper implications than the 'sins of the flesh'. And so, when we hear or read today of a 'moral breakdown', we know that the phrase refers to a major social situation involving, or seen to involve, a wide spectrum of behaviour, ranging from crimes of violence to drug-abuse to petty but persistent juvenile delinquency.

It is indeed to be counted for gain that as Christians we no longer regard lust as the primal deadly sin, or that our society does not put a premium on sexual respectability as the essential public virtue. We must admit, however, that any list of 'what's wrong with society today' will, in Ireland at any rate, place crimes and misdemeanours involving sexual activity in a position of high priority. There are several reasons for this, but I'm afraid that the most compelling is to be found in the inherent attraction of the subject. It is no accident that the word *sexy* has come to mean 'exciting, fascinating, tempting' (*Chambers Dictionary*, 1993).

There is of course much more to it than that. The liberalisation, trivialisation, commercialising – however we look at it – of human sexuality is undoubtedly part of the cultural revolution which began in this country in the early sixties (though it could be foreseen a decade earlier), and has not yet spent itself or subsided into a new 'normalcy'. Some would even say that here was the spark which set off the rest. This is, I think, far too simple a reading of what happened, but the sexual element, long concealed or controlled, has been certainly a very serious factor in the coming of radical social change.

Moral malaise

In the run-up to the referendum (November 1996) on amending the Irish Constitution in the matter of the rules governing the granting and withholding of bail, since all the Dáil parties (excepting the solitary Green deputy) were in support of the amendment, a rare dissenting voice was that of the Irish Bishops' Commission on Justice and Peace. This was articulated by their president, Bishop Eamonn Walsh, one of the Dublin auxiliaries. Their reservation was later endorsed by Archbishop Desmond Connell.

The archbishop stressed the importance of public debate on such an important issue, and then went on to say:

> 'My principal concern, however, goes deeper than reform of the law. I do not believe that we can succeed in revising present trends towards lawlessness and crime, unless we tackle the weakening of moral convictions which lies at the source of our current malaise.

> 'This is largely the responsibility of the church. But the work of the church is rendered more difficult by sustained attack on its moral teaching in so many areas of public discourse ...'

Dr Connell's remarks deserve careful consideration on two counts. First, in pointing to 'the weakening of moral convictions' as lying at the root of 'our current malaise', he clearly suggests that the perceived breakdown in public morality is real and radical, and demands a radical response. Secondly, he assumes that this response must come 'largely' from the church, with the assent and support of society as a whole. And, however problematic either proposition or both may be seen, they represent an approach to our current situation which transcends the all too partial, not to say fragmented, diagnoses and prescriptions of our political leaders.

Is it all true then? Is Irish society in a state of moral collapse, are the old values no longer upheld, do the generations which have come to maturity since the second world war consider they owe nothing to the imperatives which their elders honoured and mainly obeyed? It would be too much to expect a general consensus as to the answer, but a fairly widespread idea that 'something is very wrong' does certainly add up to what the archbishop calls the 'current malaise'.

Not everybody will point to the same symptoms. For some, the great problem is the prevalence of drug-abuse, and the apparent ease with which the pushers can market their wares. For others, it will be juvenile lawlessness and petty crime. Many will point to a perceived increase in serious crimes of violence, including rape – which inevitably leads to what will be seen as the fundamental breakdown in sexual morality, ex-emplified in broken marriages, single parenthood, unstable 'partnerships', as well as the even darker areas of prostitution and child abuse. And even the least liable to 'shock-horror' feelings must be concerned at the emergence in Dublin, and perhaps elsewhere, of the professional killer, the gun for hire.

One development on which there is general agreement is that rural Ireland is no longer crime-free. Perhaps it never was, but while the incidence of some serious offences is still more common in the urban environment (especially in Dublin and other large cities), those living alone in remote areas, particularly the elderly, have good reason to fear for their lives, and for their often pathetic property. And, while only a sentimentalist would imagine that sexual crime has been common only in cities, one has the impression that it has become more frequent and more barbaric in rural areas than heretofore.

Or, is it the case that such incidents are now reported more often, and in greater detail? Indeed one must raise similar questions regarding a whole range of offences, in both town and country. The most obvious category that comes to mind is child-abuse, including incest. It must appear highly unlikely that this is something which has developed only in very recent years. I am not thinking now so much of paedophilia in the strict sense (I mean the compulsive and often recurrent activities of the sexual deviant), but of the far commoner crime of the 'normal' individual to whom the child is merely an accessible sex object – often within the family circle.

Crime and its causes

Obviously any reliable assessment of the reality of a perceived breakdown must depend on reliable statistics over a wide spectrum of behaviour. The difficulties of achieving anything approaching a complete statistical analysis are patent – reluctance to report certain incidents being the most obvious – particularly in attempting patterns of comparison over a period of years.

However, a few figures, selected from official reports may give us some points to what's been happening. The first have to do with the birthrate. In 1987 there were a total of 58,433 registered, of whom 6,347 were born *outside* marriage, or 10.9% of the total. Six years later (1993) the total had fallen to 49,456, and the outside-of-marriage figures had climbed to 9,664, or 19.5% of the total. For the *first three months* of 1996, the total was 12,749, of whom 3,139 were outside of marriage, nearly 25%. This last figure included a total of 191 born to mothers under 18 (seven being 15 years or under) – only four being married. While it is probable that there was, by any definition, an element of criminal activity involved relating to many teenage births, it may not have been seen as such by all concerned.

As to 'serious crime' in the terms of the annual Garda

Commissioner's report, crimes against the person will be commonly and very properly regarded as the most serious. In this category, the total recorded for the year 1986 was 1,883 (1,487 detected): these figures rose to 2,035 and 1,629 for 1987, but fell to 1631 and 1348 in 1990. In 1995 (the last year for which, at the time of writing, we have complete statistics) the number of offences reported had risen only to 1663. Of these offences, 43 were murder; 10 manslaughter; 94 wounding (endangering life); 425 assault (including wounding); 9 dangerous driving (causing deaths). But figures which stand out from the page are 191 rape of females and 604 sexual assault on females or males. (There are smaller figures for varying degrees of sexual offence).

Enough to give weight to the fears and perceptions of what some of us would call a moral breakdown. Of course what can be fairly described as crime, not just breaches of traditional morality, is the main preoccupation of the several calls for 'action'. What that action should or could be remains problematic. I don't think we've gone quite the distance of the 'flog 'em and hang 'em' brigade across the water, but quite a few of our moralising commentators, and more significantly our politicians, seem to be on the way there. Already, presumably with a view to the next general election campaign, hoardings carrying law and order slogans from the main opposition party have been appearing in city streets.

'We'll make sure crime doesn't pay. And criminals do', shouts one of these warning voices. 'We'll give crime a hard time', claims another. The fact that such words can give little comfort to those who have suffered or are vulnerable to criminal depredation, is I suppose not really relevant: they proclaim a tough, no-nonsense approach, likely to please those who believe that our society is 'soft on crime'. Hardening the bail laws might seem a step in this direction, but anything beyond that is left vague. Practical ways of 'giving crime a hard time' are left to the imagination. Meanwhile, the Whitaker report on crime and punishment has remained on the shelf for years … apart from the proposal to set up a Prisons' Board, which pressure of events has led to being adopted.

Another slogan, 'Hard on crime and the *causes* of crime', has not been taken up here, as far as I am aware. The phrase was I believe coined by one of the British Labour Party's – sorry! one of New Labour's – bright boys and girls, and it has been taken up with acknowledgement by the Tory crime-bashers, or rather those of them who would wish to appear socially conscious and sympathetic to the 'economically disadvantaged' *sc.* victims of market economics.

At least it does concede that crime and criminals may have an 'unfortunate' background. What to do about it is a different matter. As that perceptive social and political commentator, Dick Walsh, has suggested in his *Irish Times* column, crime is shorthand for a series of deep-rooted problems on which there is little or no agreement:

'In fact there's a wide and growing gap on the origins and prevention of crime, though it's less evident among politicians than between other leaders of opinion – bishops and broadcasters, militant campaigners against drugs, and trade union organisers.

'On one side there are those who see crime as a single, simple issue: how to catch and keep the criminals with little thought for their rehabilitation, and less for the conditions which helped to make them as they are.

'On the other side, stand those who believe that the real challenge is to change the conditions in which crime thrives and some criminals prosper. But this approach is far from simple, and, if taken seriously, it would lead to change in many areas ...'

Walsh lists some of the areas: health, welfare, education, investment planning and environment, as well as the administration of justice. It would all, of course, mean more public spending and state investment, and the result would be long-term: there would be few if any over-night improvements. And he adds that 'for decades, politicians have shied away' from such a strategy.

He notes with approval recent contributions to serious thinking on the subject from Catholic church sources; thus Bishop Christopher Jones of Elphin:

'From my own experience of working in social services I've seen that most crime comes from the impoverished, overcrowded, underserviced concrete jungles.

'Young people there are born into a culture of crime, they are born losers, they haven't a chance from the beginning.'

I doubt if any of us would disagree fundamentally with this view. It is, of course, true that not all 'born into the culture of crime' persist in it. It is also a fact that some criminals began life in families and neighbourhoods not at all disadvantaged. Indeed, to ignore this may lead to thinking in terms of a 'criminal class,' an attitude which has led in the past, not to a greater understanding of crime, but to so labelling whole sections of society.

There are parts of Dublin, Limerick and other Irish cities and towns which have gained something of the reputation of no-go areas. Decent young men and women born and brought up in these areas have often found it impossible to secure employment, once the name of a street or district is mentioned.

Which of course in no way invalidates the unfortunate truth of what Bishop Jones is quoted as saying. On the contrary, it adds even more weight to his observation and to the need for taking it very seriously indeed. Sadly, as Dick Walsh comments, neither this approach to the problem, nor its practical implications for public policy, have become part of our political discourse on crime, its prevention, and how to deal with it as it occurs.

Faith and morals

But if such an approach were adopted and supported, financially and otherwise, as an integral part of public policy, would this in itself solve the problem? Is it, in other words, to be seen as purely a matter of social economics: Or do we need to probe more deeply, and, in the words of Archbishop Connell, tackle 'the weakening of moral convictions' which he sees as a root problem in our society? I believe we do, not as an *alternative* to socio-economic policies, but by way of arriving at a cogent diagnosis, and pointers to the way forward from our 'malaise'.

It may be noted that not alone in Ireland are moral convictions perceived to be at risk, as we approach the end of the second Christian millennium. The West as a whole is seen to be affected in this way and, in England particularly, an alleged decline in ethical values is clearly a matter of serious concern. There too, church leaders have been involved in the debate: interestingly, the Roman Catholic bishops have been stressing social justice as an essential factor in maintaining a morally healthy society, and their contribution has been respectfully received in many quarters.

But while many secular voices continue to see it as part of the churches' duty to give a moral lead, it would be foolish to imagine that any but a minority of the present generations in Britain are likely to conduct their lives *expressly* in accordance with Christian precepts or traditions. There are still areas of life where the common secular perception of what is good matches that of church teaching, but many other areas (notably in regard to sexuality) where it does not.

And I would argue that to ask whether, or to what extent, this is also true here in Ireland (or even among first generation Irish abroad) is a timely question, and one crucial to our self-understanding and to any social prognosis. I might put it like this: do faith and morals still, as the song says, go together 'like the horse and carriage'?

Or, again like the horse and carriage, are they just a pair from the past? It is a question which goes to the heart of the matter of this book. In a previous *Exploration*, we looked at the diverse but related realities of faith, religion, and religious culture, and were, I think, led to the conclusion that, while all these are alive and fairly well in Ireland today, the third seems definitely in sharp decline; the second is going through a process of change, slimming-down, and possible renewal (reform?, purification?); and the position of the first (the deep centre of the other two) is somewhat problematic in extent and influence, but still strong in essence.

Christians hold that faith is God's free gift and remains so, however conditioned by cultural circumstances, however enhanced or diminished by family or communal tradition, or by the influence of peer-groups. But all these may and do, in their several

ways, strengthen or weaken or modify the link between what we believe and how we behave – or how
we 'ought' to behave. And, sadly, they have all com-
bined (and not just in our time and our society) to
stress the negative imperatives of Christian living,
rather than its far more fundamental, positive message: the 'don'ts' rather than the 'do's'. And so the
great commandment enjoining love of God and
neighbour has too often been overshadowed by an
emphasis on the grosser breaches of that precept, and
the sanctions which these must earn. More recently,
fear of these sanctions has lost its cogency, and, with
it, what had become to many a purely negative code.

It is hardly surprising that *religion*, in its ancient sense
of a 'binding force', should have long been on the
wane in modern society, particularly though not exclusively in the Northern world. The Romans, and
perhaps other civilisations before them, recognised
the value of such a force in establishing and maintaining an obedient and docile *plebs*. Today indeed, one
has read and heard tributes to the importance and
usefulness of religion, any religion, from this point of
view, expressed by political and social leaders and
thinkers to whom genuine religious values are of no
consequence. The 'opiate of the people' is an idea still
alive and well in quarters where other Marxist insights would be anathema.

But it is not an idea to recommend itself to those who
take religious faith seriously, whether of the Christ-

ian, Jewish, Islamic or other traditions. Has then religion a role to play, as we set to 'tackle the weakening of moral convictions,' to quote Archbishop Connell? Our answer must be certainly in the affirmative, but, we would insist, not that ascribed to it by those who see it as a useful agent of social control. What then is its role, or more precisely as far as Christians are concerned, what is the role of the church? Not, we would again insist, that of moral legislator to society as a whole – certainly not over the range of discrete human and social experience – still less that of moral policeman.

So while we would be grateful for church leadership in our 'current malaise', we would, with respect, demur from the archbishop's statement that the moral task, which he so clearly identifies, is 'largely the responsibility of the church', if only because it may be wrongly interpreted as relieving our secular institutions of all but minor responsibility in the matter. Obviously, the socio-economic dimension, whose importance we have noted, is essentially the state's job. The state and other secular agencies have also a major part to play in the development of civic education, leading to the inculcation of a civic ethic, 'a sense of what it means to be a good citizen' – the lack of which is identified by our essayist, Anne Looney, as one of the gaps in our social fabric. Clearly all this, far from excluding the church's moral leadership, must enhance it; already some of the most radical thinking in the area of social justice and human rights is coming from that direction – from bishops, collectively and individually (as in the very pertinent remarks of the Bishop of Elphin quoted above), and from such agencies as the Commission for Justice and Peace and the Conference of Religious, as well as in the more informal pronouncements of pastors, theologians and Christian social thinkers.

Church and conscience

But here it is important to stress that the church's moral responsibility and function do not end with preaching and teaching, with offering advice and counsel. For the church is much more than an institution: as a moral body its membership extends far beyond the ranks of those who lead and offer direction. The rest of us may listen and learn, and it is good we should do so. But our personal and collective responsibility doesn't end there.

What can be involved in moral decision-making – which may well affect more than our individual lives – is well exemplified in Anne Looney's perceptive comment on the divorce referendum, and the challenge it offered to each of us, but especially to those with what we would regard as strong religious convictions. It was above all a challenge to *conscience*, which in turn offered a challenge to our intelligence and will. How we respond to this challenge may well be the key to the quality and maturity of our faith now and in the future, and to that faith in its relation to our moral responsibility as members of Christ's body.

In this volume we would wish to explore some aspects of the challenge and of our potential to respond to it. What our contributors have to say will be particularly relevant to the Irish context, but, obviously, much of it may be of wider application.

Anne Looney's approach is that of one deeply involved in the practice, as well as the theory, of religion teaching. Her experience leads her to an unblinkered view of moral attitudes among the learning generations, but her conclusions extend to a much wider range of Irish society, in these final years of the century and the millennium. As we have noted, she raises some disturbing questions in relation to conscience and moral choice.

The whole area of the individual conscience in relation to the teaching church, and indeed a general survey of the religion-morality ground, is considered by Fr Sean Fagan, a Marist priest and moral theologian (author of *Has Sin Changed*?) who has had extensive pastoral and teaching experience in Ireland and abroad. His contribution, complete in itself, also provides a foretaste of his forthcoming wide-ranging study, *Does Morality Change?* (Gill & Macmillan), whose title speaks for itself.

Our third essayist, Terence McCaughey is an ordained minister of the Presbyterian Church who teaches in the theological department at Trinity College, Dublin, as well as in the Department of Irish there. Antrim-born, with a deep interest in Northern

Irish affairs, he is also a past president of the Irish Anti-Apartheid Movement, and is chairman of its successor, the Ireland-South Africa Association. His concern with questions of justice, peace and reconciliation in a divided society, is reflected in the title of his book, *Memory and Reconciliation*, a study of 'Church, Politics and Prophetic Ministry in Ireland'. In his contribution to the present volume, he develops the argument of one of the chapters of that work, 'Conscience as Consciousness of the Other'.

If I might be allowed to comment on this, I would want to welcome what I regard as a very valuable reminder that the appeal to conscience, and such response as we may make to that appeal, need not and should not ever be seen as a retreat into individualism, or a by-passing of the community, especially the Christian community. It should not be necessary to stress this, but such misunderstanding is, unhappily, by no means rare among Catholics. And, ironically, while the insights and pronouncements of the Second Vatican Council should leave us in no doubt as to the essential role of the Christian conscience, the Council's very emphasis on *communio* and human solidarity has been misinterpreted as undervaluing personal decision and moral initiative, which remain vital to the church's mission.

It is also appropriate that we should be reminded of the role of conscience at a time when, after twenty-five years of armed conflict in Northern Ireland, there has been what can be described as a hardening of the moral arteries, not only in the North, but throughout the island. Even the uneasy aftermath has been marked by many incidents of deliberate and savage cruelty in the so-called punishment beatings perpetrated on both sides of the northern divide. It is worth noting that similar savagery has been a recurring feature in 'non-political' acts of violence in many parts of the Republic.

'An End of Innocence'

These examples of inhumanity have become so common that they barely evoke more than a vague feeling of disapproval and distaste: we who read or hear about them are hardly more appalled than the perpetrators themselves, our sensibilities have so far become blunted. Too long a sacrifice has, indeed, made a stone of the heart. It is then hardly surprising that this moral numbness should, after so many years, have infected our minds and attitudes in relation to a whole gamut of behaviour, which would have appalled us beyond measure thirty years ago.

It would, of course, be an over-simplification to pretend that the years of political violence alone are responsible for 'weakening' our moral convictions, but they have undeniably contributed heavily to the blunting process. Nor can we lay the responsibility of this solely at the door of the 'men of violence' and their collaborators: political action and inaction, rights denied and licensed butchery are all part of the story. But so too are moral flabbiness and a lack of political will, which allowed the rest of us to do nothing.

However, my wish is not to go over old and barren ground, but rather to suggest that we are in a position, not unprecedented in our history nor in that of other peoples, sometimes described as 'reaching the end of an age of innocence'. The phrase was used of the Americans after the disastrous Vietnam adventure, of the Swedes on the assassination of a prime minister, of the French when forced to face the facts of collaboration and war crimes; it may be used now about the Belgians, following the scandals of 1996.

I have never been happy with the phrase. It begs too many questions about innocence and about those presumed innocent. But it is a rough and ready way of indicating that peoples, as well as people, go through periods of moral change, or rather of an increasing or declining moral awareness. One might cynically suggest that the latter has been the more common: this may well be so, though I believe that there have been times when events have had the effect of forcing a new or recovered sensitivity on those who have experienced or observed them at close hand. I cannot claim that this has happened in the present instance.

Unlikely though it may seem, there may be something of gain in this. At the very least, few of us dare take refuge anymore in the comfortable clichés with which we used to prop up our crumbling patriotism. And, though our reaction to the latest atrocity may be equally conventionally expressed, it is, if we have anything of honesty left in us, uttered with a grim realisation that we are unlikely to do anything about it, even if we could. And if the sexual abuse, often violent, of women and children and the handicapped, evokes no more meaningful response, at least we may be honest enough to admit that there but for the grace of God ... Is a certain bleak honesty then, all that we may have retained or gained in exchange for our 'lost innocence', or rather, the weakening of our moral convictions? It's not much, but it's something.

We may learn to face the fact that as the world changes, and it clearly does, so do we. We may learn to accept this change in ourselves, and live with it, and with all those other changes around us, however unwelcome or uncomfortable or even frightening they may be. I believe that in all this we may find both challenge and a certain reassurance in Sean Fagan's essay, *To Live is to Change.*

Change gives us a rich invitation to a living and positive morality, which can enrich our own lives and the lives of others. We can contribute, in communion and solidarity with our fellow Christians, to the life and mission of a changing church. But this personal contribution of ours is not *for* the *church*, but through the church, for the world, for humanity, for everyman and everywoman, who is our neighbour.

'Individualism carries within it the seeds of its own destruction: it just doesn't work.' So writes Garret FitzGerald in the essay which completes the present *Exploration*. It is the mature judgement of one who continues to observe and assess the development of Irish society, to which he has himself made a very considerable contribution. And he does well to remind us that 'Christianity is above all a social religion.'

I suppose the true Christian word for morality is charity, or, preferably, Love – driven and powered by Faith and Hope. Can we accept the challenge of this message, this mission? Can we communicate it across the 'generation gap' and the other gaps and even chasms which divide us? Our answer has to be that of the apostle Paul, who saw clearly that of himself he could do nothing, but in him who sent him, he could do everything.

CHAPTER 2

The Moral Chasm: Across the Great Divide

Anne Looney

The Enniscorthy *Guardian* of August 25th 1935 reports on the closing sermon given at a retreat on Our Lady's Island. The chosen text of the celebrant, Fr Murphy, M.SS, was 'He that loveth danger shall perish in it'. The preacher, believing, like all good homilists, that a current context was important in order to keep the attention of the congregation, referred in his sermon to the recent Criminal Law Amendment Act and the new 'crime' of offending decency. He praises the Free State government for taking action against the 'scandalous conduct' of young people with their 'craze for semi-nakedness', particularly in the seaside towns of Wexford. Fr Murphy saves his greatest praise, however, for Benito Mussolini who has 'put the promotion of morality in the forefront of his programme'. Fr Murphy continues:

> 'What is the cause of this modern laxity of morality in Ireland that has necessitated drastic action on the part of the state? I shall tell you. We have a foreign press pouring monthly, weekly, even daily, pages and pages of indecency. In pictures, in text, in paragraphs, are given forth ideas utterly at variance with Catholic princi-

ples. What would have shocked our forefathers no longer shocks.'

What would have shocked our forefathers no longer shocks … Some sixty years after Fr Murphy preached his sermon, I was sitting at a parents' meeting exploring the theme of handing on the faith. All agreed that this was not an easy task. The conversation at the coffee break turned to the broad issue of trying to teach children right from wrong. One of the parents observed that there are two little words every parent dreads to hear. She explained that these two dreaded words are usually delivered by an adolescent or pre-adolescent to a parent at the end of the aforementioned parent's painstaking explanation as to why certain behaviour is unacceptable. These two words deal the parent a killer blow and undermine any moral authority they thought was theirs. The words? *'So What?'* Subsequent to that meeting, parents of teenagers have noted a trend, confirmed by enquiry among the teenagers themselves, to truncate these two words into a far more lethal *'So?'* Apparently, the correct tone to adopt when delivering this to a parent is to draw out the syllable with an upwards inflection at the end. Accompanying body language can include looking at one's watch or the door or straightening one's hair. Eye contact with the parent is to be avoided at all costs!

Where do the beleaguered parents go from there? They may read in Sunday supplements of plans in

Britain to tackle the 'moral crisis', and long for someone to tackle the moral crisis currently wearing head-
phones in the back bedroom! They may feel that Fr
Murphy's own solution – 'greater devotion to the
mother of God ... a spirit of self-denial, mortification
and penance, that were from time immemorial associ-
ated with the pilgrimages to Lough Derg in the North
and Our Lady's Island in the South' – is worth a try,
and vow to buy their offspring the latest musical offering from the *Faith of our Fathers* stable. But deep
down they know that their best efforts are going to
lead to yet another 'So what?' And they've had about
all the so-whatting they can take!

Fr Murphy, preaching in 1935, pointed to a moral
chasm opening between young people and their forebears. Most parents in the closing years of the century
could point to a similar chasm. But it does not divide
the past from the present, forebears from current generations. Some parents find that they themselves are
on one side and their own children are on the other.
Schools can tell stories of parents 'invited' to school to
'discuss' the disruptive behaviour of their offspring,
and agree with the teachers and the principal that
their child is disruptive or lazy or unruly. Teachers
and principals have all been faced with the shrugged
response. 'We've tried. There's nothing we can do.
She/he is the same at home.' And the tone is one of
resignation, even of despair. In parents, and indeed in
children, there is an increasing awareness of the gap,
a sort of moral chasm, between one generation and
the next.

'The Moral Maze' was something of a catchword in the eighties. It was used to describe the difficulties of discerning right and wrong in an increasingly complex society. The classical image of the paths of good and evil, and right and wrong – an image popular in morality plays and fairy stories was amended to reflect the fact that straight highways were not to be found in the eighties. Instead the eighties were littered with hard cases. Tricky situations. Lesser of two evil dilemmas. School text books for religious education (the focus of most moral education, and more of this anon) were full of hard cases ... man hangs over cliff ... injured friend is attached by a rope ... if he doesn't let go the rope both will die ... what does he do? This type of scenario was common. Apparently the moral maze is littered with injured mountain climbers and their worried partners! But our mountain climbers were something of archetypes for the moral maze. Finding your way through tricky situations was good moral exercise.

No entry?

But the image of moral maze is of little consequence in a post-modern context. We can no longer presume that the maze has a mutually agreed entrance point and an exit, that there are boundaries within the maze which cannot be crossed. We can no longer assume that people are willing to enter it in the first place. The image of a *chasm* is perhaps more useful for the age in which we find ourselves. This image presumes difference and division. It locates the challenge of morality, not in the sorting out of hard cases, but in establishing that there is a morality in the first place. And that this morality should impinge on human behaviour.

When I studied moral theology, the image of morality as *call and response* was 'big'. Christian morality was a call from God and the faithful person answered that call in word and deed. Morality sprang from one's relationship with God. Immorality was the refusal to enter into, or the determination to end that relationship. In the cold light of the nineties, this seems too cosy an image. Sort of snug and intimate. Because for many, the moral chasm has brought a very real experience of crying in the wilderness and exposure to extremes never thought possible. This new moral chasm has cut a swathe through the generations, isolating one generation from the values of the previous one. The term 'lost generation' used to apply to disaffected and alienated young people. But the moral chasm has ensured that few, if any, feel the security of being 'found'. We are all a little lost.

But perhaps the chasm image leads to excessive pessimism? Surely bridges can be built? There can be reaching across the great divide. Is it not overly bleak to assume that the lines of moral communication have been completely severed? It is true that reaching across does happen. For some adults, for example, the lines of communication pose little difficulty. Parents, for the most part, know what they want for their children; they want them to be happy, to be independent and self-reliant, to have friends, to be involved in productive work, to feel relaxed, to be loved and assertive. And when it comes to values they want their children to be honest and truthful, to be loyal, to share, to be unselfish, to be good citizens, to be fair, to trust and be trustworthy. Parents know that this is what they want for their children and so they attempt to send the right message across the bridges between the generations, the bridge over the river *why?*

But any bridge which may be built can be clogged with a bewildering array of alternative values and messages. The messages of parents may not easily pass. While some still communicate with ease, there is a growing number of parents who find themselves facing the great *So What* moment!

The image of a moral chasm could give rise to the notion that adults have, to use a well-worn phrase, the moral high ground, while the hapless youth inhabit one of the lower reaches of Dante's inferno. Parents know, but their children don't. Parents have developed moral maturity while their children remain in a sort of moral infancy. Parents can discern the right and wrong about which their offspring seem to be so confused

But, as most parents and adults know (and politicians can be included in both categories), such moral high ground exists in myth and legend. The post-modern adult can end up clinging perilously to the cliff edge at times. One may be sent over the top by increasingly complex situations which make the injured mountain climber and his friend seem straightforward by comparison. Another may be at a loss to explain why something should or should not be done. 'Because it isn't nice.' 'Because I say so!' 'Because it is illegal!' Or the classic 'while you live under my roof, you will obey my rules'! How many parents have found themselves driven up the chasm wall, or even over the precipice, by the *So* of an obstinate teenager?

Now, many adults will themselves remember having such statements delivered to themselves, and accepting them with more or less good grace because they were spoken with authority. Authority is a challenging concept of the nineties. Where is it? Who has it? Who has the kind of authority that carried the mystique, the wisdom and power that produced, not blind obedience, but willing obedience out of a belief that a certain behaviour was for our own good. (And while we may like to believe that all was obedience in the past, consider whether Fr Murphy's words *did* lead to less semi-nakedness on the beaches of Wexford!)

Churches? Do they have any authority any more? Agencies of law enforcement? Schools and teachers? Government? Where is the weight of authority now? Ask people under eighteen where is the authority they respect. Who are the people they admire? What are the influences of significance in their lives? The worlds of sport and music offer ephemeral icons to some. Influential peers also have their roles. Some will point to people in political power or to their parents. But, the deeper into the morass of disaffection and social alienation one goes in Irish society, the more deafening will be the silence of the response to the question of authority.

The Buzz

I once asked a bored class of fifth-year students, who seemed beyond enlivening, whether they felt that they were the authors of their own lives ... people who make things happen as opposed to people to whom life happens. Did they see themselves as simply the passive recipients of all that was dished out to them by life? I asked the question tongue-in-cheek in an effort to raise them from a torpor which seemed to be impervious to even the most creative teaching methods! I reminded them that I was fifteen years older than they were, yet seemed to have far more energy than they did. I waited for their indignant response, for the burst of rebelliousness that would assure me that the generation, which would celebrate its coming of age with the beginning of the new millennium, had some fire in its belly. But their fatalism caught me off guard. They said – with one exception who said that she did have moments when she felt in control, but they were not *school* moments – that they had no control over their own lives. One said that she felt like 'a rubber duck in someone else's bath', a metaphor that may lack literary merit, but does get the point across. Talking with other teachers, it appears that this fifth-year group is not unique. Youth workers working outside the formal educational structures will name the same ennui, especially in areas of social deprivation. Many will point to the fact that 'facilities for youth' has become something of a cliché in the nineties. Young people don't want facilities. The youth clubs are empty of over-fourteens because hanging around 'is a *better buzz*'. In the seventies and eighties, 'drop-in' centres were all the rage for disaffected youth. But all the disaffected want to do is to drop out. Dropping *in* is the last thing on their minds. The depressing film *Trainspotting* must be the definitive description of this culture of nihilism at its most extreme. *Choose Life* is one of the film's slogans in an ironic twist of the anti-abortion chants of the eighties. Choose life. Life has no purpose and then you die. So choose an enhanced form of life. Take drugs. They may kill you. But it's a better buzz.

I wonder at the source of this fatalism, this near resignation. Where does it come from? I am sure much thought will be put into its source in the months and years ahead as we too move inexorably to the kind of crisis in public morality now gripping Britain. Psychologists and sociologists may engage in in-depth research and provide statistically supported answers. I can only go on my hunches! One of those hunches leads me to support the theory of Fr Murphy on the negative influence of the 'foreign press' or the nineties version of it, television. It is akin to flogging the proverbial dead horse to lay the blame for any ill of society on top of the television remote control. But my concern about television does not arise from the values or non-values it presents, but from its very domination of Irish family life. Now I already feel that I sound like my mother, if not my grandmother, on the 'dangers of television'.

When I began teaching twelve years ago, I used to be surprised at the influence television had on what the students would write in English class. In my day (on which side of the moral chasm am I?), we wrote essays about outings and adventures with Blytonesque rescues and lashings of ginger beer. Now, in reading an essay, I am likely to have to quell my queasiness as a headless body is eaten by worms and gallons of blood splatter the fast food joint. That the visual imagery to which the students have been exposed has influenced their writing is indisputable. What is frightening is their lack of any critique of those images. And their inappropriate use in an essay. There are no consequences of such violence. It is merely *there*. Students haven't been influenced by these images. They have absorbed them.

Even television *viewing* is too optimistic a term for what happens in many households. It is television *observing*. Irish comedian, Kevin McAleer, wasn't far off the mark in recalling years sitting watching the television and occasionally turning it on! Viewing implies some sort of subjective involvement and critique, but this is becoming rarer and rarer in young people – indeed it is fast disappearing from the adult population

as well. Television 'viewing' has become a solitary activity – check the figures for multi-television households, with the teenage bedroom being the favoured
location for the second set. And the notion of watching anything in its entirety has gone out the window.
Flicking is in. Narrative structure is out. The enter-
taining image is what television is for. And entertainment is everything.

I call it entertainment. So would you. But to today's
teenagers it is 'part of the buzz'. Getting and having a
buzz is everything. It is the only relief from the mon-
otony of passive resistance described by that group of
fifth-year students. Short sharp burst of highly colour-
ful MTV is good. So is the drug Ecstasy, because it
helps to have more fun for more time. And more fun
is better.

I remember when the Liverpool child, Jamie Bolger,
was abducted and killed, the Archbishop of Liverpool commented that the wave of revulsion and hor-
ror expressed by parents was not simply because the
little boy could have been theirs. It was a recognition
that the abductors could just as easily have been their
children. In classroom this proved to be an available
learning moment. Classes were shocked by what had
happened, and their shock lay in the recognition of
themselves, or a part of themselves, in the killers of
the young boy. How far will you go for the buzz?

Television and its indiscriminate absorption help
support the culture of the buzz. And unwittingly,

many adults have themselves contributed. Of course, there is our ambivalent attitude to the use of alcohol which sends all sorts of messages to younger generations about the *need* for a buzz. But such messages have been given for years, without leading to the kind of more-ism that currently exists. What is new, is the more-ism of rampant consumerism.

No matter what we have, there is always something more to be acquired and, it goes without saying, a new place to buy it. For adults in the prosperous classes, having is everything. And the goal of all – be they union members, employers, farmers or social welfare recipients – seems to be an increase in disposable income. Saving or borrowing for the something more seems to be the new opiate of the people – those with jobs. It has certainly boosted a whole new set of places at which to worship at the altar of consumerism. And, from those new shrines to shopping, emanates a crystal-clear message. Having is good. Having more is better. Having as much as possible is the key to happiness.

Personally I cannot help but feel that, when this message reaches the bored and passive and limited-income younger generations, it translates as 'Having fun is good. Having more fun is better. Having as much fun as possible is the key to happiness. Get the buzz.' And when the message of the muezzins in the marketplace echo in the neighbourhoods where there is little or no disposable income, it translates as

'Having is good. Having more is better.' And if you can't have ... well the path to goodness and happiness is closed to you.

In describing one side of the moral chasm, generalisations abound. But they ring true. Yes, there are groups of young people committed to action for justice, involved in environmental activities in their local communities, working for and with marginalised individuals and groups. But the growing trend is towards the fatalism of the bored, the passivity of the disaffected, for whom nothing matters. And if nothing other than the buzz matters, then moral decision-making is a process increasingly alien to this generation. It is not that they are cut off from a coherent values framework. It's just that these are the values of selfish hedonism, rampant consumerism and the primacy of the buzz. Decisions made in this context look senseless to those standing on the other side.

Towards moral adulthood

And what of those of us on the other side? The adult generation. And there are several generations among us. We are not a homogeneous group. Among us are those who long for the days of age-old certainty, when moral decision-making was done by the wise and virtuous. Because Ireland (or most of it) was something of a mono-culture, those dictates were largely those of the Catholic Church. That day is over. And its passing leaves two gaps in the moral framework of many adults. Firstly, Ireland missed out on

the development of any sort of civic ethic. We didn't
need one, when the morality of the Catholic Church
was espoused by everyone. People respected the
property of others because it was a sin not to.
Stealing, murder – all of those happened, but they
carried the sanction of eternal damnation – which
may have been something of a deterrent! And in a
society like ours, without any apparent ethical sense,
it seems that only deterrents work. Drink driving became something of a social leprosy when there was a
greater chance of getting caught. Thousands of people disappeared from the live register when there was
a crackdown in social welfare fraud. Millions were
collected in the tax amnesty.

Sanction, however, is a very shaky moral foundation
for any society. There must be a vision, a sense of
what it means to be a good citizen. We never had such
a vision. Being a good Catholic was enough! So the
decline of organised religion exposes our lack of a
civic ethic. But a far more serious gap is also exposed.

This gap was most tellingly revealed in debates pre-
ceding the divorce referendum, a difficult time for
most Irish adults. Most of us knew people who were
separated, or living in miserable marriages, sustained
only by the need to save face. Most of us knew that
we didn't want a country which embraced a cavalier
attitude to marriage. Many people had religious ob-
jections to divorce. There were strong arguments on
both sides. Then the Catholic Church offered its guid-

ance – 'inform and follow your conscience'. Now, while individual bishops insisted that this informing conscience meant following church teaching, the overall message appeared quite threatening to many adults. It sounded like they were being told to weigh up the options and *make up their own minds*. This was, to extend the metaphor of the fifth-year student, like pulling the plug on the rubber ducks!

For years Catholic adults had been told how to behave in even the most intimate details of their lives. Now we were being challenged with a serious moral decision ... and I am convinced that many of us hadn't got a clue how to go about making that decision. Because this was a new task: making a decision that would have consequences for future generations and being asked to take responsibility for it. The day after the referendum a new Ireland dawned. It did not dawn to the sound of the shredding of social fabric or the clatter of the horsemen of the apocalypse pounding across the ancient cobblestones of Hibernia. It dawned on the beginning of moral maturity. In many ways we have been children. Adulthood had begun. And it would have begun, I feel, regardless of the result: in terms of moral maturity it was the painful process and not the outcome that counted.

So the chasm does not simply separate an alienated and bored youth population from their morally mature elders. Adults no longer inhabit the safe, secure world of moral certainties. As a nation we are not good on moral leadership. We love Irish solutions for Irish problems. Where the rest of Europe is tackling the thorny issues of genetic engineering, of in-vitro fertilisation, of the meaning of death with dignity, we seem to still inhabit a sort of nod-and-wink world – if we don't ask, well why should it bother us? But these issues will bother us sooner or later, and once again our moral mettle will be tested.

And so one side observes the other across the great moral chasm. Adults look at future generations with something akin to despair. They give great sighs of 'we were never like that'. They are often frightened by the sheer disregard for the values of their forbears that seems to be the hallmark of those on the other side. And, of course, they look with great hope to schools. Every time there is a radio or television de-bate about the state of the nation's youth – about drugs, drink, crime – name your problem – it only takes about thirty seconds of airtime before someone tells us that 'it's all down to the schools' or 'we need to develop programmes for schools'. But schools do not operate in a vacuum. Teachers know that they may teach something *ad nauseam*, but real learning will not take place unless the same message is heard *outside* the classroom walls. As adults, we seem to be entirely unconscious of the message we send. The messages that say 'spend!' And the messages we suc-cumb to, in the enthusiasm with which we embrace the age of multi-media.

And the younger generations look across at their fore-bears and hear the jumble of messages echoing across the great divide. And amidst all these messages comes the cry of all forebears, 'Be like us!' No challenge there! We are not asking them to join the ranks of the morally mature, of the formed and forming con-sciences. We are not inviting them to shoulder the burden of moral responsibility for one's actions – local and global. We are not calling them to face the complex issues of bio-ethics and technology. We can-not invite them to such tasks, for we are ourselves only coming to terms with the invitations to moral adulthood.

CHAPTER 3

To Live is to Change

Sean Fagan SM

In spite of the odd moment of nostalgia for a romantic Ireland that never really existed, most people reflecting on the state of the country would happily admit that overall we are in a much better position than ever before. Health, education, job opportunities, the possibility of foreign travel and so many other benefits make life comfortable for most of our people in a way that was unimaginable by previous generations. The country has changed enormously in just a few short years, and there is no indication that it will not continue to change. But while rejoicing in our better standard of living, many people will be upset by what change has done to our society. For their consolation they need to be reminded of Cardinal Newman's wise words: 'To live is to change, and to live fully is to change often.' Change is an essential part of life. The challenge is to recognise it and to adjust creatively to it in order to grow in maturity.

But the negative changes can be upsetting, making us fret for the future. Anne Looney's description of the moral chasm dividing parents from children will resonate with the many parents who feel helpless and frustrated in their attempts to have their children accept the values of faith and morals that were the backbone of society when they themselves were growing up. One can only sympathise with these parents, faced with a seemingly impossible task as they try to hand on to their children the Christian faith which nourished their own lives. They wonder how can they cross the moral chasm that seems to separate them from the children they cherish. Any attempt at dialogue brings as much response as shooting into cotton wool. The 'So what?' shrug is a most effective conversation stopper. When parents seeking help look to the church, the authority that was such a support for their own faith, they find that church leaders are just as helpless as the parents themselves. But worse still, very many parents are shocked to discover how deeply the church is hated by their children. They know that this vehement emotional reaction to what the teenagers have learned of recent scandals is not a reasoned position of principle, but it is still a shock for many parents.

Anne Looney's account of her classroom experience is a concrete example of the perceived breakdown in Irish society which Seán MacRéamoinn so well describes in terms of morality and religion. The problem is not restricted to teenagers. Surveys of university students show that they are under tremendous pressure, but the majority cope reasonably well. Some experiment with hash and ecstasy pills, but in general they tend to stay away from harder drugs. Large numbers have no qualms about sexual activity, with an easy attitude that would shock many parents. But counsellors helping them say that in general they have a responsible outlook. A typical comment from an eighteen-year-old girl is: don't have sex with a partner unless the relationship has lasted for at least six months, and always take precautions, using either the pill or a condom. Students generally reject the popular perception of them as careless, irresponsible, promiscuous. While not adhereing to the strict rules expected by parents with regard to sex, they claim to be serious and responsible in their relationships. This is a considerable change in the moral climate of young Ireland.

New attitudes

An indication that the change of moral climate is also to be found among adults are the words of Social Welfare Minister, Proinsias de Rossa, about cohabiting couples with children. Responding to the interim report of the Commission on the Family, which recommends that such couples should be treated as a 'family' for tax purposes, he said that we must accept that in Irish society we have a wide variety of family types, and that the traditional form of the family based exclusively on marriage is no longer the only one. He argued that there should be no discrimination against couples who have families outside marriage. This is a major change in attitude from the times when such couples would be ostracised and penalised. A further example of the change of moral climate in the country is the Family Law (Divorce) Act, effective from the end of February 1997, which is intended to help some of the 95,000 people whose

marriages have collapsed. By the way, Minister de
Rossa also added the sobering reminder that the
country has to come to terms with the fact that, in
some cases, families can be institutions of oppression
and violence.

Seán MacRéamoinn is rightly hesitant about using
the phrase 'the end of an age of innocence' to describe
what has been happening. He prefers to note that societies or whole peoples, as well as individual persons,
go through periods of moral change, or rather of increasing or declining moral awareness. I think this is
quite true, but it is part of the larger phenomenon of
social and cultural change which has always been a
feature of human history. In a certain sense, what we
are experiencing in this change is normal and under-
standable. One could very responsibly say of it, 'So
what? What else is new?'

This can be both consoling and challenging. It is consoling to know that the phenomenon is quite natural,
that there is no need to panic. But it is challenging in
so far as it shatters our complacency and calls us to a
deeper, more critical faith and a more convinced and
personal morality. In other words, a faith and a
morality capable of meeting the challenge of our new
culture. From the moment when our human ances-
tors first began to wonder about the world in which
they found themselves, religion has always been the
quest for, and the celebration of the deeper meaning
of life. But it was never an abstract, a-historical, a-
cultural experience. It was always rooted in, and ex-

pressed through, a particular culture. The bible itself, as God's own word, is a living word, and so it must become incarnate, take flesh, and come alive in each new culture. The question is: how can this happen in the culture that is taking shape before our eyes?

A better world

In spite of the disturbing picture that emerges from the accurate reports of our two chroniclers, it is simply not true that the world is in a worse state now than ever before. Many aspects of the contemporary scene can sadden parents who think nostalgically of the tranquil faith and ordered morality of their own youth. But the myth of the golden age is as old as human history. It is easy to imagine that things were better in the past, that we are now further off from heaven than when we were growing up. But if we can leave aside the nostalgia and take off the rose-tinted spectacles, we might remember the darker side of our history: the poverty and restrictions, the conservative atmosphere that censored creative thinking, the emphasis on authority and obedience that left little room for honest questioning, the fear that prevented any serious rocking of the boat, the kind of church teaching and discipline that made it difficult for people to develop a mature conscience. One or two generations ago, there was none of the extreme violence, drug abuse and sexual promiscuity that provide today's media headlines, but it is difficult to measure the degree to which this was the result of deep faith or moral conviction. Social conditions were different, sanctions were stronger, and, for many people, the possibilities for serious wrongdoing were extremely limited.

For most people in Ireland today, life is so much better than it ever was. Thank God for that, but the changes have gone further than material improvement. Many of them have resulted in cultural changes to society itself. Formerly these cultural shifts were subtle and slow-moving, only recognised with hindsight. But the speed of change has grown enormously during recent centuries. Indeed it is no exaggeration to say that the world has changed more in the past fifty years than in all of previously recorded history. Today's world is as different from the 1920s as the 1920s world was from that of Julius Caesar or Jesus of Nazareth. The vast majority of the goods we use in daily life were developed only within our own lifetime. Plastics came in the 1940s, transistors in the 1950s, computers in the 1960s, microcomputers in the 1970s, biotechnology and genetic engineering in the 1980s, and the present decade has seen the explosion of information techniques, giving instant access to unlimited sources across the globe. Each new invention seemed to be just an improvement on what went before, but in fact several of the discoveries radically changed human life. When the printing press was first developed, it was seen as a speeding up of the process of copying by hand. But in fact it radically transformed human life in so far as it became possible for vast numbers of people to have access to the printed word, which transformed education. The railroad and the motor car were first seen simply as faster and more comfortable means of transport than the horse, but in fact they introduced major social change, particularly the car, with the increased mobility that enabled people to work in one place, live in another and take their recreation in a third. The ease of travel enabled people to break out from their immediate social environment of family, village or town. The anonymity of modern cities provides an escape from the pressures to conform that can inhibit personal freedom, but it also removes the support, example and challenge of our familiar community when it comes to preserving traditional values and making difficult moral decisions.

Culture change

With our God-given creative intelligence we change our material environment, we have new experiences, and we are continually changing ourselves. Moral responsibility remains a constant, but how we exercise it in terms of discernment, decision and action cannot abstract from the fact of change. Pre-modern or traditional society tended to remove the burden of choice from individuals, but large areas of human life, previously determined by fate or community tradition, are now seen as occasions of personal choice for people. Improved health, higher and more general education, rising living standards, the growth of feminine consciousness, and urbanisation, are material and social factors which altered people's ways of thinking and feeling about themselves and their world. The alteration amounted to a culture change which impinges considerably on morality and religion.

Culture is used here not in the popular sense of the intellectual or civilised development of an individual who can be described as a person of culture. It refers rather to a wider and deeper reality, so that a person can be said to belong to a particular culture. Culture in this sense refers to a people's whole way of life, their social symbols and rituals, art, language and literature, social relationships and groupings, and especially the particular way of thinking that guides their decision-making in economics, politics and morality, as well as in religion. Culture includes all the meaning systems of a society. It includes religion, although religion seeks the deeper meanings of human life. Culture is a set of meanings, values, models and patterns incorporated in and underlying the actions and communication of the life of a particular human group or society. This ideology is consciously or unconsciously lived by the group as expressing its own human identity and reality. It is learned and passed on from one generation to the next. It grows and develops as it is passed on, in so far as each generation modifies it in the light of its own experience. At the heart of every culture is a worldview, a way of looking at the world and all of reality. People's whole value-system stems from this way of looking at things. Morality and religion reflect and express a people's culture, and they are always coloured by culture, since the cultural background affects all dimensions of human living.

A totally new culture

Today's youngsters are living in a culture that is radically different from the one in which their parents grew up. They have to cope with pressures far more subtle, more powerful and more complex than those known to their parents, and they are faced with a vast variety of choices that were simply undreamed of in the past. There is simply no way of comparing generations in any worthwhile way because the context has changed so radically. The parent who begins a lecture with the claim, 'when I was your age …', is liable to be told by the teenage son or daughter, 'but you were never my age'. It is true that the parent was once a teenager, but it was in a very different world, a world long since dead, never to return. The chasm described by Anne Looney is not just an age-gap between two generations, but a vast culture-gap not easily bridged. There are no simple answers or magic solutions, but the strategy of the three A's may be helpful: Admit, Accept, Adjust. Admit the reality of what is happening, accept it as natural, and adjust creatively to it in the light of our Christian faith and of all that is best in our tradition.

The first step in bridging the chasm described by Anne Looney is to admit that it is there. It is quite real between parents and children, but it is even greater between youth and the institutional church. Young people know that there is a vibrant new culture in Ireland today. For so long we were a struggling, degraded people, poor and depressed. We have made so much progress in a short few years. Irish music and literature is acclaimed around the world as never before, even in the most unlikely countries of the Far East. Our economic performance has overtaken that of many European countries, and we are highly regarded in the world of computer technology and software. The new affluence has brought enormous possibilities of choice for many people. All this has meant freedom, a better life, more opportunity for pleasure and enjoyment. We should be proud of our achievements and grateful for our good fortune, but at the same time we must never forget that 30% of our people still live on or below the poverty line.

However, it has all come so suddenly that we may have lost our balance along the way and too easily lost sight of enduring traditional values. But church leaders, and many parents, seem to focus on this negative aspect and they condemn all of modern culture as negative. Young people picture the church as a kill-joy institution, saying an automatic 'No' to everything new, shouting 'Stop!' at every new experiment. It can easily give the impression of being an oppressive body, not listening, not learning, not wanting to hear. In some public debates, it seems more concerned with power and control rather than with moral influence, and moral authority, and it finds it hard to accept powerlessness. Church leaders who condemn the new culture give the impression that the church is somehow neutral, above culture, apart from history, sitting in judgement. But the church is not simply surrounded by alien cultures, but of its very nature must be a part of culture. The problem is that the culture that shaped our contemporary church is no longer the dominant culture, so that the traditional church is still imprisoned in the old culture and has difficulty in being the *Church in the Modern World* so well described by Vatican II.

Of course, the culture change that has taken place in Ireland in the last few years is part of the change that has been going on in the wider world. During the past few decades, we have been going through one of the greatest culture changes in our entire history, involving a whole new outlook on reality, and reaching into every detail of experience. Thirty years ago, the Second Vatican Council adverted to it:

> 'The accelerated pace of history is such that one can scarcely keep abreast of it ... and so we substitute a dynamic and more evolutionary concept of nature for a static one, and this results in an immense series of new problems, calling for a new endeavour of analysis and synthesis' (*op. cit.* n. 5).

Part of the problem in today's church is that people talk about religion and morality and how they can be taught, with practically no reference to this culture change. But the change affects both our notion of religion and morality and our views on how they can be 'taught'. It is taken for granted that there is a revealed and timeless morality that has only to be prescribed or handed on, but in fact there are question-marks over the meaning of morality, its content and how it can be passed on to others. So many people look to the past, or to some revelation from above, as the source of moral teaching. But life is not as simple as that.

The call to responsibility

It is significant that, even in the area of dogmatic truth, our truths of faith, the Vatican Council speaks of revelation as an ongoing process, continuing into the present. It says that 'Christ reveals us to ourselves' and gives meaning 'to the riddles of sorrow and death' (*op. cit.* n. 22). 'Believers, no matter what their religion, have always recognised the voice and the revelation of God in the language of creatures' (n. 36). In revelation, 'God spoke according to the culture proper to each age' (n. 58). Speaking of revelation as a continuing process, to be newly expressed for every age in prophetic witness, the same document says that *'it is the task of the whole people of God, particularly of its pastors and theologians, to listen to and distinguish the many voices of our times and to interpret them in the light of the divine Word, in order that the divine truth may be more deeply penetrated, better understood and more suitably presented'* (n. 44).

This last quotation has been highlighted because of its special significance as an ongoing call to the whole church, not just its leaders. It is not a mere pious exhortation, but a challenging call expressed by the church's highest authority, that of the Pope in solemn

council with the bishops of the whole world and ad-
dressed to all God's people. Seán MacRéamoinn
rightly praises Archbishop Desmond Connell for
clearly identifying the weakening of moral convictions as the root cause of the moral breakdown in
today's Ireland, but he would have some hesitation
about the statement that the moral task is 'largely the
responsibility of the church'. No doubt it is no more
than a Freudian slip (from our centuries-old Catholic
subconscious) that gives the impression that the
church is simply its appointed official leaders. The
council documents continually speak of the whole
people of God as the church. It certainly does that in
the above quotation. It is the whole body of Catholic
believers who are to be involved in the process of listening, learning, discerning, interpreting and pre-
senting the divine truth, but it is particularly the task
of leaders and theologians.

This subsidiary clause, linking pastors and theologians, has an added importance today, as a corrective
to the recent tendency on the part of the Roman
Church to censor and punish theologians who have
been faithful to their centuries-old traditional task of
creative reflection on the truths of faith in the context
of changing cultures. Sadly, the message conveyed in
recent years is that theologians are expected to be
mere public relations people, protecting and promoting decreed truths. Many high-ranking theologians
today are laity and quite a number are women.
Unfortunately, the laity, who make up the bulk of the

church, are seldom consulted by church leaders, and there are no meaningful structures in place that would enable them to participate in the task. The serious and considered views of many married lay people, based on their lived experience, were totally ignored both in the writing of *Humanae Vitae* in 1968 and in the 1980 consultative Synod of Bishops which dealt with family life.

The silent majority

The experience of not being listened to, of being rejected in the area of their special expertise in the field of married and secular life, has left many Catholics so angry that not a few have drifted away from the church they loved. But even those who did not directly have this experience of rejection would find it difficult to respond to the council's call to involve themselves in the task of making God's word more meaningful in today's culture. The simple reason is that the institutional church for far too long kept its people dumb. Is it not strange that at a time when Irish Catholicism is being threatened as never before, so few ordinary Catholics speak up? How many can give a convincing account of the faith that is in them? How many can make a worthwhile case for Catholic morals, as distinct from repeating, and being asked to defend, the 'teaching' handed down by their leaders? For too long Catholics were spoken *for*, more often than they spoke in their own name. They did not lack interest, intelligence or commitment, but they were seldom encouraged and practically never had the structures to make worthwhile communication possible. More seriously, the majority of them were not provided with the confidence, the language or the knowledge that would equip them for critical thinking. The over-emphasis on 'church teaching', in a context of authority and obedience, prevented any serious questioning, or drove it underground. Even in the wake of Vatican II and *Humanae Vitae*, when people were told to follow their conscience, they were reminded that it had to be an informed conscience, with the implication that church teaching would provide the information. Unfortunately, some felt this was simply the old 'do as you are told' attitude, and they wondered why there should be any reference at all to conscience if this were the case.

A first step in bridging the chasm between parents and children is to close the gap between the 'institutional church' and God's holy people in general. There are so many people in Ireland, both young and old, who are still solidly Catholic and happy to be so, but they would be more happy if they could have a fuller experience of being the church. They need to be affirmed, healed and enabled to grow. They need to be trusted so that, in turn, they can trust their own God-given intelligence and common sense when it comes to making moral decisions. They need to have the liberating truths of Vatican II, not forgotten in documents seldom seen or preached, but reflected in every official church proclamation and decision, and lived out in practice in the church's day-to-day life. They

could be freed from inhibiting fears if they knew a little more of the church's chequered history, as a struggling pilgrim people on the way, being gradually led
into truth by the Holy Spirit. They could be consoled
by the enormous amount of human weakness and sin
in that history, but also encouraged by the abiding
presence of God's love, forever breaking through.

Adjusting to change

It would be a liberating experience for people to re-
alise how much the church has changed down
through the centuries. The 'Rock of Ages' image is a
misleading myth. The church's function is to preach
in word and deed the good news of the gospel, and
the freedom we have in Jesus, and to live out his commandment of love. But how this commandment is to
be understood and implemented will depend on our
human experience and our culture. While remaining
essentially the same in all cultures, it has found different expressions in different situations. People need to
know that there have been radical changes in the
church's teaching through the centuries. There is no
shortage of examples, with regard to slavery, property,
usury, war, women, sexuality, marriage, responsible
parenthood, organ transplants, social justice, church-
state relations, conscience, conscientious objectors,
freedom, human dignity and peace. It is a false loyalty
to the church, and no loyalty to truth, to pretend that
all the changes were minor modifications. Changes
on all these subjects were substantial, indeed radical,
and in some cases recent changes actually contradicted
what went before.

When change occurred, it was not the result of a special revelation from on high, nor something decreed by pope or bishop, but as a result of God's holy people getting new insights, through their experience, into the meaning of the gospel. The official formulation of church teaching should reflect this. In fact, in the area of revealed truths, the Pope can only define what is already the faith of the church, of the people. In the area of morality, the lived experience and Christian wisdom of God's holy people are essential to the discovery of truth, and they should be told this. They should know that truth cannot simply be decreed, but only discovered, shared, explained. In fact, *the church has never made an infallible statement on a matter of morals.*

In our moral decisions we can be guided by the accumulated wisdom of the church expressed in its teaching, and, more often than not, our own decision will be in line with it. But when it happens that, after careful study and reflection, we come to a different conclusion about what is the responsible thing to do in a given situation, we are bound to follow our conscience. Loyalty to conscience is loyalty to God. We may later discover that we were mistaken, but even in error we have a solemn duty to follow conscience. Of course, we need to form our conscience, not with prepackaged answers, but with an appreciation of and attachment to basic human values, with the habit of being faithful to conscience in our actions, with the practice of serious reflection on all the factors of a situation, trying to understand them, reason about them, foresee possible consequences, get advice when necessary, and then, in the light of all this, to make a responsible decision.

There are two extremes to be avoided: making frivolous, uncritical decisions in serious matters and claiming that we are following our conscience (which is nonsense), and on the other hand, lacking the courage to listen to our deeper experience and then launch out in freedom once we have made a responsible decision. Conscience is intensely personal, but a conscience-decision is never made in isolation. It will generally reflect our background and culture, the values of our family and Christian community. The Vatican Council expects the church to help people to grow as free persons, to encourage personal responsibility and moral maturity. It says that the church ought to 'form people who will be lovers of true freedom, who form their own judgement in the light of truth, and direct their activities with a sense of responsibility'. People need to be encouraged in this direction. They will begin to believe it when they feel trusted and respected.

Conscience is sacred

The council speaks of the sanctity of conscience, describing it as a sanctuary, a sacred place where only God can enter. Is this our attitude towards people who differ from us? Moses took off his sandals when he felt that he was on holy ground. If we had the same reverence for the conscience of other people, it would enable them to grow. St Paul often speaks of 'the glorious freedom of the children of God' (Rom 8:21), and Jesus promises that if we obey his teaching we will know the truth, and the truth will set us free (Jn 8:31-32). If more people in the church, through the experience of their membership of God's holy people, could experience this inner freedom, they would be happy in their own skins, at home in their faith and in their culture, and be better equipped as peace makers and bridge builders to reach out to all in need.

The purpose of this chapter was not to solve the problem of the moral chasm described by Anne Looney, but hopefully the above reflections may be of help to people concerned about it. One thing is certain: lecturing or condemning is counter-productive. A first step is to create an atmosphere of openness and trust in which younger people feel valued and affirmed. Our Christian faith tells us that each one of them is infinitely precious, created in the image and likeness of Jesus, destined for eternal happiness. We may not use these particular words, but we should encourage them, affirm them, recognise their basic goodness and tell them over and over again that we believe in them. Tell them how good they are, and if this is true and we tell them often enough, they may come to believe it. There is no question of turning the clock back. For many people the old culture has gone. The challenge to the church (meaning all its members, not just the leaders) is to read the signs of the times, understand the new culture developing before our eyes, recognise the many aspects of it that are in harmony with the gospel, and enable the good news of God's word to take flesh in this new culture, so that God's word may be truly a word of hope, of love, of life.

Trust

It would be a pity if the first two chapters of this book were to be interpreted as suggesting that Ireland is in a mess, on the way to perdition. We have our problems, quite serious ones, but God's holy people have always encountered problems in their centuries-old history and managed to survive them. There are hundreds of thousands of good people out there, old and young, teenagers and students, with a real awareness of the supernatural, with a deep and solid faith, and with a great attachment to the best elements of our Catholic and Irish tradition. Let us thank God for them, make space for them, and especially in today's critical, questioning world, let us encourage them to proclaim the faith that is in them. We need to find ways in which they can be strengthened in their faith by sharing it, in local groups, leading ultimately (but not too quickly or superficially) to a true national assembly of the people of God. Today's negative image of the church needs to be replaced by the joy and hope that shine forth from the Vatican II vision of it. When Jesus appeared to the first believers after his death and resurrection, his greeting was, 'Peace'. But more than once he asked them, 'Why are you afraid?' We need to get rid of our fear, and one way of doing this is to feel that we are trusted. We need to trust each other more. Too many of the laity feel that they are not trusted. With all its preaching and multiplicity of words, the church can too easily forget that the only way to trust people is to trust them.

CHAPTER 4

Conscience

Terence McCaughey

An MRBI survey published in mid-December 1996 found that only 29% of Roman Catholics made up their minds on what were called 'important matters' by reference to the church's teaching. The others followed their consciences. It was an interesting statistic, but of course, as so often with statistics, it raised almost as many questions as it answered. What, for instance, constitutes an 'important' matter? Is the Pope's teaching on birth control more or less important than what he (or, for that matter, in Ireland, the Justice 'desk' at the Conference of Religious) has to say on poverty and the redistribution of wealth, on which the majority have for years made up their own minds? And, even more importantly, when people say that they follow their consciences, does this mean that the church has had no function in helping them to inform their consciences prior to voting or marrying or taking whatever action is involved? After all, whatever other pressures the leadership of the church has exerted on the faithful, it has always been the church's teaching that conscience is sacred and takes primacy over all else.

It is the inalienable right and responsibility of each person 'created', as the author of Genesis puts it, 'in the image of God', to inform themselves of the facts of the case and then stand up and say 'Yes' or 'No', and be prepared to take the consequences. The 'conscience' in Walt Disney's film, *Pinnocchio*, is represented as a diminutive figure who guides and warns the hero and, in the end, vulnerable and tiny as he is, saves him from the consequences of his errant behaviour. Without making exaggerated claims for Walt Disney as theologian or philosopher, we may nevertheless say that he has captured something very important about conscience, i.e. that it seems to us like something which is ours yet operates upon us more or less from the outside. We 'respond' to it.

One young person who was asked recently, 'How do you understand the word "conscience"?' said in reply, 'I think my conscience is formed by older people or parents or by people I respect.' No doubt, this is and always has been a significant ingredient in that monitoring system we all carry about with us under the name 'conscience'. Sometimes we accept what we have received from the elders, but other times what we receive is modified considerably. The dogmatism of the elders in some cases, or a gradual diminution in their credibility, leads to our questioning their values and their assumptions. Both dogmatism and diminished credibility have undermined the authority of the clergy in Ireland, particularly over the past decade, without any doubt.

The formative authority of older people in our

processes of assessing the circumstances and making moral decisions can also be diminished as we ourselves become aware of circumstances and factors which we come to suspect they have not taken into account. So we have said, as many young people now undoubtedly say of us, that the elders are not 'with it' or are unaware of what it is like 'out there'. They are seen, possibly as well-meaning, but often as ill-equipped for the task of informing our consciences or aiding our decisions. This phenomenon was graphically described twenty-five years ago by Margaret Mead, in her book, *Culture and Commitment, A Study of the Generation Gap*. She was by then a senior figure, and her book was the result of her sensitive relationship with students less than half her age in the heady days of the sixties in North America. That experience, added to the insights she had gained from decades of fieldwork as an anthropologist, led her to question the assumption, which she attributes to the 'adult generation', that values have a timeless quality, or are only fractionally modified by the passage of time. She notes the extent to which 'technological innovation' brings about alterations in cultural character.

The innovations in technology and in the forms of institutions of the past fifty to a hundred years are so great, she argues, as to have created a situation in which 'the idea of orderly developmental change is lost for a generation of young, who cannot take over what their elders are doing now'. Margaret Mead, by 1970, had come to see children as facing 'a future that is so deeply unknown that it cannot be handled ... as a generation change ... operating within a stable elder-controlled and parentally-modelled culture.'

In her book, she traced a movement in societal development from (1) what she called 'post-figurative' societies, in which children learn primarily from their forebears, to (2) what she called 'co-figurative' societies, 'in which both children and adults learn from their peers', to (3) that type of society which is becoming increasingly dominant throughout the 'developed' world, i.e. the 'pre-figurative' culture, 'in which adults learn also from their children'. 'Until very recently,' she writes, 'the elders could say, "I have been young and you have never been old." But today's young people can reply, "You have never been young in the world I am young in, and you never can be."'

Change and the churches

The churches in Ireland have too often shown themselves unwilling or incapable of taking on board the extent to which technological innovation has changed the world we live in, and even the way we relate to one another. The Roman Catholic Church is perceived simply as saying 'No' to every innovation – particularly within the field of medical and genetic research. That refined capacity to distinguish between things which are not the same, which was a hallmark of much of the best theology of the past, seems, rightly or wrongly, to have been lost to a *magisterium* which, for instance, lumps together contraception and abortion. A fastidious preoccupation with the use or non-use of condoms in the face of an AIDS epidemic can only provoke young people of integrity and high-mindedness to ask, 'Are you serious?' A situation has developed whereby the apparently incredible character of the church's teaching in this area leads to its teaching in all areas scarcely being heard.

When will a church in this country, which has taken the scourge of AIDS and of drug addiction seriously, have the courage at least to address the challenge to legalise cannabis and other 'soft' drugs? (This has been advocated by the Franciscans of the Merchants Quay Project in Dublin's inner city.) Simply lumping 'soft' and 'hard' together – often without reference to our centuries-old experience of alcohol – is to run the risk of appearing not to appreciate how serious the situation is. Here the experience of responsible young people must be listened to closely. In many such areas, however, we adults are (as again Margaret Mead suggests) a little bit like pioneers in a new country or continent, who build their house according to plans brought with us from the 'old country'. Once the house is up, the young may complain that the windows do not keep out the draughts or the floor keep down the rising damp. The result is that father and mother must listen to this reasonable complaint and, together with the children, work out ways to build that take seriously the climatic conditions in the new continent. Sometimes (perhaps often) this will commit the older people to the task of teaching their children, not *what* to learn, but *how* to learn. This would involve, and (if humankind is to survive) must involve a learning together – which is an interesting and relevant phrase when one reflects that 'conscience' comes from a root, *con + scientia*, a common or shared knowledge. It becomes a shared sense of how things are, and how, in the face of that, we may perhaps behave.

Both Catholic and Protestant Ireland retained the essential characteristics of post-figurative culture until very recent times, that is, a culture in which the young learn largely (exclusively?) from the old. Pockets of post-figurative society survive here and there still, and it would be largely true to say that the churches are organised largely on the assumption that we still live post-figuratively. Even where that does not survive in its full vigour, the past has a more powerfully continuing role, both creative and destructive, in the present, and in our decision-making about the future, than a synchronic anthropologist like Ms Mead would readily allow. What we commemorate, and what we choose to forget, influence our present and our planning for the future.

Faced with a world bewildering in its complexity and the plurality of its options, many people will and do simply opt to remain (if possible) within the old 'postfigurative' way. This is, no doubt, in large measure the explanation for the growth of dogmatic sects, and furnishes at least part of the explanation for the fact that Archbishop Lefevre's seminary in Paris is full of students while the ordinary seminaries of the Roman

Catholic Church in France are calling out for candidates. However, opting for the dogmatic certainty offered by such institutions, and the formation of conscience within these constraints, is not likely to be favoured by more than a small minority. One rather hopes not.

A large number of people today live with a foot in more than one camp. For practical purposes, it may be mostly from our peers that we learn to work out what we should or should not do. But, when the going gets tough (as in social crises, war, or under a totalitarian regime – as in parts of Eastern Europe during the period of Stalin), people will find solidarity and strength in sticking to what has always been done – learning from the elders. But in a situation such as obtained in this state in the 1950s, where the influence of a powerful and monolithic church was still to be felt everywhere, there were always those who nevertheless made up their minds on important matters largely by reference to their peers. Such people were not seen as being 'good Catholics', but even to acknowledge that was tacitly to accord to church teaching an unduly normative character.

One suspects that one or two later generations plodded along like this – according to the 'traditional' teaching of the church an authority it did not enjoy in practice. So, for instance, those who in practice disobeyed papal teaching on birth control could either 'confess' their disobedience from time to time, or find a priest who, as it was said, 'understood'. This *modus*

operandi held for a time. Then, quite suddenly, it did
not – sometime after, the discipline of regular auricu-
lar confession lost its grip. Perhaps the threat of purg-
atory, and even hell, was in decline.

Protestants, whose preaching had been given urgency
by instilling fear of an endless eternity of torment re-
served for those who had not accepted the Lord Jesus
Christ as their personal Saviour in this life, also lost
power – though at a different rate and in a different
way. But those who persuade people to right action
by frightening them are not helping them to develop
their consciences, as Francis Xavier knew well, when
he wrote the hymn:

> My God, I love thee not because
> I hope for heaven thereby;
> nor yet because who love thee not
> are lost eternally.

One wonders whether the contempt which many
young people, reared as Christians, appear to feel for
their forebears' religion, and their hatred of the
church, is the contempt and hatred that we feel for the
giant or the ogre that frightened us last night but, in
the daylight, is seen as no more than a shadow on the
wall. The church, which truly has been the 'cracked
vessel' of the gospel, is seen by a disturbing number
of young people as a power-hungry scam which has
lost the teeth it scarcely needed to bare in its heyday.
These elders, for reasons fair and unfair, have for
many lost their credibility as formers or informers of
conscience.

So what is this thing we call 'conscience', which it seems we must develop for ourselves? this thing which is part of us, yet distinct from us? this sense of being responsible, not only to ourselves and those around us, but even (beyond that) to that 'Other not ourselves that makes for righteousness', as Matthew Arnold put it. What is the Christian understanding?

Conscience and consciousness

Even to begin to answer these questions, we do well to recall that, for instance in French, the word 'conscience' means what in English is denoted by the word 'conscience', but also by the word 'consciousness'. Indeed, in the early Christian literature, the Greek word we translate as 'conscience' most often means 'consciousness' – consciousness of how things really are, how they are in God's sight and, therefore, in the end, will be. And it means consciousness of the other – whether we mean the transcendent Other we call 'God', or other people, or that material other we call 'planet earth'. We cannot live without a developed sense of all these or without developing that sense. We dare not plan without reference to them. 'Informing conscience' is one way of describing this process of developing the sense of the other – whether that Other is the one Christians have learned to call 'God', or other people or the world. The subtle interplay of these had been well articulated long before the time of Jesus or Paul, in stories which do not, in fact, use the word 'conscience' or 'consciousness'.

The twin stories of the aftermath of the fall of Adam and Eve and the aftermath of the murder of Abel by his brother Cain make the point. After the fall of Adam and Eve, the two are represented as attempting to draw a curtain between one another and between themselves and God. But God seeks them out; walking in the cool of the evening, the Lord God calls out to Adam who is hiding away in the trees, 'Adam, where are you?'

After Cain, the son of Adam and Eve, has murdered his brother, the same voice calls out to him also. But this time the question is, 'Where is your brother?' The triangle of the self, the Other and the others, binds these two stories together as, in fact, it also forms the framework of the human condition. The two relationships are not to be separated, but neither are they to be collapsed into one another. In the Cain and Abel story, Cain kills his brother, not because he hates him, but because Abel's sacrifice appears to be more pleasing to the God Cain loves than his own. Abel's presence is intolerable because he stands between Cain and the God he loves and loves to please.

Holding together, and yet apart, the obligation to the Other and to the others, without whom we cannot live coherently, is itself the exercise of conscience, in the biblical understanding. Consciousness of the others as others, who are alien to me and yet indispensable and (more difficult still) also loved by others and by God, is the refinement and informing of conscience. Then comes the further recognition that we are defined by one another as well as by God, the Creator and Saviour. So men are by women, the strong by the weak, the well by the sick, the straight by the gay, Protestants by Catholics – and vice versa in each case. This means, of course, that we are all called to make that imaginative leap whereby we no longer think and legislate, speak and write, as though the group we belong to were in itself the norm, from which others are an unfortunate or deliberate deviation.

If we are right in thinking that this consciousness of the Other (with a capital 'O'), and of the others, has evaporated in whole tracts of our society, so that the answer to any kind of moral exhortation is, as Anne Looney records it, 'Get lost!' or 'So what?', then we must, I think, ask about the truth of those claims we make for Ireland as a close-knit society. If under 30% vote in a referendum, as was the case in the most recent one, and if less than 30% of voters ever cast a vote in any election in (say) West Dublin, then we have to face the fact that for a large number of our fellow-citizens (a majority?), there is no sense of the institutions of state, or even local government, being theirs. The spectacle of those who are participant in those institutions, either running them (as it must appear) for their own advantage or actually plundering them, can only serve to sink that majority deeper in the mire of cynicism. To talk to the alienated about developing a consciousness of the other is meaningless, just as Sean Fagan reminds us that hectoring and lecturing are useless.

In a lecture delivered in Dublin in November 1996, Justice Albie Sachs of the Constitutional Court in South Africa described how those who had been given the task of drawing up a constitution for post-apartheid South Africa tried, at every point, to involve as wide a spectrum of the whole people as possible in the process. The Constitutional Court, of which he is a member, is there to keep watch on legislation drawn up under that Constitution, but also it attempts to be as easy of access as possible so that citizens can make claims directly to them on rights they believe them-selves to have under the terms of what is, after all, their fundamental law. How far it will succeed, only time will tell. But, in the meantime, we can say that it is a brave attempt to give constitutional expression to the truth that all citizens are indispensable. If we are to recover something of that sense in our society, we have, as a matter of urgency, to take the political steps necessary to recover for the disadvantaged and the alienated a sense of ownership.

Inclusiveness

We have already observed that, in the earliest Christian understanding, and in a continuing tradi-tion ever since, 'conscience' has been understood to involve 'consciousness' – in particular, consciousness of others. The fact is, however, that many of those others are and will remain (even to the most informed and imaginative conscience) more or less alien. Still others will be strident, difficult and unlovely as a re-sult of their suffering, poverty, illness, or as a result of the discrimination they have endured on grounds of religion or race or gender. Their suffering has not necessarily made them beautiful or admirable, but they are there just the same. It might be more accurate to say, they are *here* – with us.

For, however much we wriggle or avert our gaze, the others are ultimately not avoidable – no matter how effectively our social policies may ghetto-ise them in great sprawling housing estates or high-rise flats. The Ulster Protestant is not always a winsome figure, but (s)he is *here*, not 'up there'. The recognition that the others are here, not over or out or across there, changes everything. When a member of the community is beaten with batons and has legs broken, or when a bomb goes off, or even when a bomb is primed, something dies a little within those responsible. What dies (and perhaps has to die if the bomb is ever to be made ready) is conscience – consciousness of the mundane ordinariness of those whose death it is designed to bring about.

It has been said that politics is the art of minimising the number of your enemies. But that saying means that politics, at its best, aims to persuade as many as possible so that as great a consensus as possible is created. It does not mean that you marginalise those who do not fit in or are surplus to the requirements of your economic plan – much less does it mean eliminating those perceived to be alien or to be standing in the way of 'progress'.

Christians, in spite of their patchy record in this field,

should be to the fore in insisting on this kind of inclusiveness. After all, two of their primary affirmations are:

(1) that there is One who created all and to whom all are responsible; who relates to all and calls us to do so too; and

(2) that there is one who engaged with the power-structures of his time and waded through its ambiguities in the name of what he called God's kingdom, and paid the ultimate price.

In this connection, it is worthy of notice, especially by Christians, that Jesus of Nazareth was put to death by the representatives of the greatest empire and legal system the world had ever known, and by those who sat in the chairs of Moses and Aaron, representing the greatest religion. The lonely road that led him to that end was neither well-lit nor well-signposted.

One last thing. We operate in a world which (no matter how clever we have become) we do not fully understand and never will, it seems. Part of the reason for that, and for the difficulty we have in discerning what we ought to do about what we think is wrong, is that we are ourselves part of the problem we wish to see solved. We have symptoms ourselves of the malady we earnestly desire to cure. So our picture of the predicament itself, and our ideas of how it may be tackled, are necessarily impaired. Nobody – whether political theorist or political practitioner or church leader – should pretend otherwise. For we now really do see the possibilities through a darkened glass. That is why we say that the exercise of conscience belongs much more to the realm of faith than of sight.

At critical and terrible times, our room for manoevre seems often to have been pared down almost to nothing. After taking everything into account, we may come to reckon that whatever we do or don't do is fraught with possible or even probable disaster. Yet something must be done. It is the plight of Ben du Toit in André Brink's novel, *A Dry White Season*. 'If I act,' says Ben to himself, 'I cannot but lose. But if I do not act, it is a different kind of defeat, equally decisive or maybe worse. Because then I will not even have a conscience left.' Brink leaves us to conclude, as indeed we must, that that would be the worst state of all.

CHAPTER 5

Society and Solidarity

Garret FitzGerald

I have a recollection (which may be factual but may, perhaps, be no more than a remembered dream!) of being interviewed decades ago on television and being asked what quality I would most wish my children to possess, and of replying, without hesitation – and also without thought, 'Vitality'. This came back to me when I read Anne Looney's powerful piece about the passivity of many members of today's youth, with their 'So What?' or even 'So...?' in response to a question about making things happen rather than having life simply happen to them.

At times in the past, reflecting on this dimly-remembered – perhaps even imagined – episode, I have felt a bit embarrassed about my response, feeling I should instead have given a more morally-oriented response. But after reading Anne Looney I felt that, if I did in fact reply in those terms, perhaps it wasn't such a bad answer after all.

Passive voices

For passivity of the kind she describes – which I can readily recognise as the attitude of a section of today's young generation – is almost sub-moral: it virtually excludes the concept of morality, for moral issues surely arise only in relation to doing, saying, or at least thinking actively about *something*.

The kind of passivity she has experienced can be totally isolating; by excluding any reaction – good, bad, or even indifferent – it interposes an impenetrable barrier against communication. A society that induces such an attitude amongst any significant proportion of its youth must be in some measure sick.

Of course, as she herself points out, a great many young people, the vast majority I believe, avoid this trap, and still come through adolescence successfully – whether as rebellious or as co-operative members of society. But many, even of the vast majority who emerge with their vitality intact, seem much less motivated to play an active social role than were those earlier generations of young people who were moved to challenge actively, and sometimes passionately, what they saw as defects or evils in the society in which they were growing up.

It may be right to attribute some of this passivity to the amount of time children spend watching television, but that is not the whole of the story. As she also suggests, the individualistic materialism that appears such a prevalent feature of the adult world around them encourages them to identify happiness – which so often is a function of relationships with others – with what might be called 'buzziness', fundamentally a solipsist phenomenon.

But we really know very little about this whole phenomenon: the process by which active small children often become passive rather than, as used to be the case, actively rebellious teenagers. Why has the need to change the world come to seem so much less challenging than was formerly the case? Why do the evils of our society today provoke fatalistic acquiescence and opting out, rather than, as in the past, stirring up dissent and rebellion? We do not seem to know the answers to these questions – and, not knowing them, are singularly ill-equipped to address the issue of youthful passivity.

It seems clear, however, that one factor at least is the absence of inspiring role models in the adult world which they observe around them. Even before our public life was tarnished by the scams and scandals of 1996, politics had lost much of its earlier capacity to attract the interest of successive generations of young people.

And the church of the great majority of Irish people has also lost its authority, even before its handling of a pent-up accumulation of previously suppressed sexual scandals. Some of this was probably inevitable with the general spread of secularisation, but the process was certainly accelerated after 1968 by what appeared, to the great majority of old and young alike, to be the irrationality and unrealism of the distinction the church authorities attempted to make between different forms of contraception; this proved fatally damaging to the Catholic Church's already weakening moral authority.

Making sense of morality

The vacuum in moral leadership left by church and state might have been less damaging if, as Anne Looney suggests, there had existed in Ireland a well-established civic morality. But that is something that never developed in Ireland amongst the majority Roman Catholic community – partly because in the pre-independence period the institutions of state were in varying degrees alien to many Catholics, commanding only limited or provisional loyalty, but partly also because then and later the Catholic Church provided such an all-embracing moral code that for its members there was no room, or perceived need, for any other.

A notable feature of Catholic moral teaching has been its insistence on authority as the source of its moral code, submerging the rational ethical basis of this morality. For Christian morality is not, of course, separate from or opposed to the rational humanist ethic that has emerged over millennia, as a necessary means of promoting the good health of society, and indeed the successful continuance of the human race itself; it is a particular refinement of that ethic, inspired by and developed from the teachings of Christ, but subject to a number of accretions that originated in response to specific ethical challenges faced during two millennia of church history.

There may have been several reasons for the reluctance to relate Christian morality to its rational ethical

basis: concern at the way some rational ethical principles have at times been distorted by self-interested in-
terpreters, or unhappiness with what may have been
seen as lacunae in this code. But also perhaps a desire
to preserve and promote authority for its own sake,
and at times also a half-conscious recognition that
while basic Christian moral principles correspond to
those of a rational ethic, many accretions to Catholic
moral teaching, developed *ad hoc* to meet past conting-
encies and never subsequently reviewed in the light
of changing circumstances, do not.

One way or the other, the result has been that remark-
ably few Irish children have ever been told, for example, that indissoluble monogamy is not just a clerical
hobby-horse, but in fact finds a powerful rational
justification in the special needs of human children to
be nurtured and cared for, over a very much longer
period than almost any other members of the animal
species. Yet, when and if put forward in support of
the churches' teaching on Christian marriage, this rational argument can readily be seen – above all by
children! – as strongly reinforcing that teaching.

Seán MacRéamoinn is understandably wary of a situation in which political and social thinkers, to whom
genuine religious values are of no consequence, pay
tribute to the importance and usefulness of religion,
as some kind of 'opiate of the people'.

But this does not apply the other way around: it does
not mean that those engaged in religious teaching

should be similarly suspicious of rational support for Christian moral principles: to me at least that seems a false corollary, and one which in present circumstances can have very negative consequences.

One of the most disturbing features of today's world, and in particular of the world of the young, is that religion for very many is not just seen as irrelevant but actually as a hostile and negative force. The religious element in the Northern Ireland ethnic conflict – recently paralleled by events in Yugoslavia – has for many Irish young people been profoundly alienating: the certainties of religion are seen, with some justification, as an aggravating factor in the bitterness of these conflicts.

If religion can be so horrifyingly divisive, how can the young be expected to accept it as a force for good? If separate education in religious schools leaves those who emerge from these establishments so deeply embittered with each other, how can churches, which purport to be Christian, justify insisting on the perpetuation of such a system? To such questions the young – and indeed the not-so-young – are offered no credible answers.

And when, like a dam bursting, the delayed prosecutions of priests and brothers for decades of paedophile offences seem to fill the papers week after week, giving a quite misleading impression of the ongoing extent of this scandal, anti-religious prejudices are powerfully reinforced.

Against this background it will not be easy to restore confidence in a purely Christian value system based on a system of ecclesiastical authority. However commitedly Christian most of its leaders and members may be, a society content to rely exclusively on such an approach for the reinstatement of the community values needed to make it work, could be making a fatal mistake.

Conduct and credibility

The deep-seated problem that now exists needs to be tackled on two levels. First of all, we now urgently need to develop, and present to the young, through the school system, a civic morality based on the incontrovertible human need for a code of conduct that promotes the long-term good of the human race, and the immediate good of the society in which they and we live. The impact of environmentalism upon the younger generation should make them receptive to such an approach – which could also alert them to the fact that the Christian morality taught in religion classes has more going for it than their hostility to authority-based teaching may have led them to believe.

The second thing that badly needs to be done is to restore the moral credibility of church and state – of religion and politics. Neither will be easy.

For the churches, there would have to be a fundamental shift back to a church of prophecy – a church challenging effectively the evils in our social order that

are as evident to many young people as they are ignored by so many of their elders.

But, for that to be done with credibility, it must be
done with authentic passion by those whose commitment to social justice is beyond doubt – but whose
critique of our economic order is rigorously based,
and thus incapable of being dismissed by economists
and politicians as 'pie in the sky'. For such prophetic
voices to be heard at the level of church leadership,
radical changes would be needed in the hierarchical
structures of the institution, and also ultimately in the
quality of those seeking ordination.

The credibility of politics also needs to be restored.
Even before recent events occurred, this credibility
was being eroded by such factors as clientelism,
favouritism by ministers in respect of their own con-
stituencies, and political patronage – confined though
this has been in Ireland to a very narrow range of
public appointments. When one now adds questions
about funding of political parties and of individual
politicians, as well as suggestions of actual financial
corruption in certain areas such as physical planning,
it is scarcely surprising that politics has been acquir-
ing a bad name. And, however unfair and unjust
some journalists' political comments may be, it is
ludicrous for certain politicans to blame all their woes
on journalists, instead of facing the need for radical
reform of the way they do their business. The time is
more than ripe for a radical re-assessment of many of
these features of our political system.

Sex and marriage

In the first chapter, Seán MacRéamoinn counts it a gain that Christians in Ireland no longer regard lust as the primal deadly sin, and do not put a premium on sexual respectability as the essential public virtue. That we have moved to a more balanced and comprehensive idea of morality is certainly a good thing. But we cannot ignore the potentially disruptive impact upon society of the scale of the changes that have recently taken place in sexual *mores* in Ireland – and in particular of the speed with which these changes have come about, which I believe has no parallel anywhere else.

For the truth is that, after many decades during which we had been most effectively sheltered from changes that were occurring in the rest of the industrialised world, we have had to absorb all these changes within the space of a single generation.

Thus before 1962, when artificial contraceptives were not readily available here and before the contraceptive pill became available, and when abortions could not easily be procured even in neighbouring Britain, less than 1,000 out of more than 60,000 births were non-marital (viz. 1.5%). And it was *not* the case that this low figure had been significantly reduced by 'shotgun marriages' of teenagers, for only 750 births in that year were to married women under 20 years of age. Clearly, therefore, the incidence of pre-marital sexual intercourse at that time was much lower than today.

By contrast, in the 12 months to June 1996, a reduced total of 52,500 pregnancies led to 11,250 non-marital births, to which must be added some 3,500 abortions of non-marital pregnancies in Britain. That represents an overall non-marital pregnancy rate of 28%, and the non-marital rate for first pregnancies is now approaching 45%.

The proportion of non-marital births in Ireland is in fact higher now than in most other EU countries – higher than in Germany, Belgium, the Netherlands, Luxembourg, Portugal, and Spain, and several times higher than in Italy or Greece. This can be only partly accounted for by a possible wider use of contraceptives and a higher incidence of abortion in some of these countries. Meanwhile age-specific marital fertility fell by 45% in the quarter of a century between 1966 and 1991 (later figures are not yet available), and for those aged 35 and upwards the decline was over 65%.

Moreover, within the past fifteen years (1981-1996), the marriage rate has dropped by over one quarter. For women under 25 the decline in the marriage rate has in fact been over 55%, but a good deal of the drop in marriages amongst this age-group reflects a postponement rather than an abandonment of marriage; at this stage it is impossible to assess the relative importance of these two factors in the reduction of the marriage rate.

These are huge social changes to have occurred over

such a very short time-scale; by any standard they involve a major and very sudden destabilisation of the traditional pattern of relations between the sexes in Ireland.

Our institutions clearly have yet to come to terms with the full implications of what has been happening. It is true that certain steps have been taken to meet new needs arising from this situation: thus artificial contraceptives have been legalised and, several decades ago, provision was made in the social welfare code for the financial needs of single mothers. Moreover, last year's divorce referendum finally recognised the need to restore a measure of social stability by providing, on a restrictive basis, civil recognition of second unions following marriage breakdown.

But, at a fundamental level, we have yet to re-assess our attitudes to this radically new situation. Thus, little thought seems to have been given to the extent to which the state's tax and social welfare codes may operate to discourage marriage – or might be modified to encourage it. And as Child Benefit is gradually raised with a view to matching, and thus making possible the phasing out of, Social Welfare Child Dependency Allowances, what will be the implications of this for the Single Mother's Allowance, which will then become more vulnerable to the accusation of being a straight disincentive to marriage?

I mention these issues to illustrate the potential social significance of the sudden transformation of Irish sexual attitudes that has occurred in very recent times.

Solidarity

But that is only one aspect of the cultural changes taking place in our society. The underlying destabilising force is individualism – a preoccupation with the individual's 'right' to self-development, at the expense, if necessary, of others. True, if others would be directly and visibly damaged by an individual's assertion of his or her rights, in most cases this will be seen as imposing some restraint on individual self-fulfilment. But there is a notable reluctance to recognise that others may also be damaged indirectly, and above all a strong resistance to the idea that people can be responsible for the cumulative impact upon society of their individual acts.

The refrain 'I can do what I like as long as I don't hurt anyone else' is seen as a let-out for behaviour which, when indulged in by many individuals, may have the cumulative effect of dangerously weakening important social constraints. Indeed, even the idea of society itself is subject to challenge, and the importance of social cohesion and solidarity is down-played.

What is often missed by those propounding this kind of individualism is that happiness – as distinct from pleasure – is a social rather than individual phenomenon. An individual may seek and find pleasure on his or her own, but happiness comes from a constructive inter-action with others: in working with them, playing with them, helping them, or even serving them. If this truth is lost, the quality of life is hugely diminished.

This is something which the Christian Church has always understood and preached. Christianity is above all a social religion: 'Inasmuch as you have done it unto one of these the least of my brethren, ye have done it unto me'; 'Love thy neighbour as thyself'. It is in mutual solidarity that people find their own value. As Terence McCaughey writes, 'Holding together, and yet apart, the obligation to the Other, and to the others, without whom we cannot live coherently, is itself the exercise of conscience ... We are defined by one another as well as by God.'

Turning the clock back is impossible; we have to live in the world as it is today. And, as Sean Fagan has said, there was much that was negative in the world in which people of my generation grew up, and for most people in Ireland today life is much better than it ever was.

But that does not mean that we have to accept the destructive reign of individualism, or accept Margaret Thatcher's self-revealing dictum, 'There is no such thing as society.' Individualism carries within itself the seeds of its own destruction: it just doesn't work. Ultimately it will give way once more to a recognition of the essential verity of human solidarity: we need each other, and it is on that basis any enduring value system must ultimately be built.

The Contributors

SEÁN MACRÉAMOINN, broadcaster and writer, is a prominent commentator on religious and cultural affairs.

ANNE LOONEY is a teacher of religion at second level. She is also involved in teacher training and curriculum development for religious education.

TERENCE MCCAUGHEY, who is a Minister of the Presbyterian Church in Ireland, is a Senior Lecturer in the Irish Department, Trinity College, Dublin, and also teaches in the School of Biblical and Theological Studies.

SEAN FAGAN, SM, is a Marist priest and lecturer in Moral Theology at the Milltown Institute, Dublin. He was Secretary General of the Marist Society in Rome from 1983 until 1996.

GARRET FITZGERALD, lecturer and journalist, is a former Taoiseach.

COLUMBA EXPLORATIONS

Columba Explorations is an occasional series in which The Columba Press aims to explore current issues as they arise in church and society. The two previous titles in the series are:

Authority in the Church
Edited by Seán MacRéamoinn
Contributors: Bill Cosgrave
Louis McRedmond
Mary McAleese
Catherine McGuinness
Terence McCaughey
ISBN 1 85607 154 5 96pp paper £5.99

The Church in a New Ireland
Edited by Seán MacRéamoinn
Contributors: Anne Looney
Gerry Myers
Carol Dorgan
Séamus Ryan
John Dunlop
ISBN 1 85607 170 7 96pp paper £5.99

If you would like to be kept informed about future volumes in this series, please send your name and address to:

the columba bookservice
55A Srpuce Avenue, Stillorgan Industrial Park,
Blackrock, Co Dublin
Telephone: (01) 294 2560 Fax: (01) 294 2564
e-mail: columba@indigo.ie